W9-DFX-051

Ripley's®
Incredible
INSECTS

Written by:
Louise A. Gikow

with an Introduction by:
Dr. David Grimaldi
Curator, Division of
Invertebrate Zoology, American
Museum of Natural History

Series Edited by:
Madeline Boskey, Ph.D.

SCHOLASTIC INC.

New York   Toronto   London   Auckland   Sydney
Mexico City   New Delhi   Hong Kong   Buenos Aires

BELIEVE IT OR NOT! WHEN THREATENED, LADYBUGS SECRETE POISON FROM THEIR KNEE JOINTS!

Developed and designed by Nancy Hall, Inc., New York, NY
Art on pages 4, 12, 15, and 20 by Ron Zalme
Art on page 5 by Leanne Franson
Designed by Tom Koken

No part of this publication may be reproduced in whole or in part, or stored in a retrieval system, or transmitted in any form or by any means, electronic, mechanical, photocopying, recording, or otherwise, without written permission by the publisher.

Published by Scholastic Inc.,
90 Old Sherman Turnpike, Danbury, Connecticut 06816

Copyright © 2004 by Ripley Entertainment Inc. Ripley's Believe It or Not!, Believe It or Not!, and Believe It! are registered trademarks of Ripley Entertainment Inc.

All rights reserved.

Scholastic and associated logos are trademarks and/or registered trademarks of Scholastic Inc.

Printed in the U.S.A.
First Scholastic printing, January 2004

ISBN 0-439-63359-1

Robert Ripley began his career as a sports cartoonist. One day, he was facing a deadline and couldn't think of anything to draw. Then he had a brainstorm. Digging through his files, Ripley found nine amazing sports facts—and finished his cartoon just in time. Little did he know it would become the first of many Believe It or Not! cartoons.

Soon, Ripley was seeking out oddities of all kinds. To find new material to share with his readers, Ripley traveled far and wide. His searches resulted in incredible facts, unusual people, strange places, unique customs, and amazing creatures from around the globe. Many of his findings appeared as cartoons in his books and syndicated newspaper columns. Others were collected in Ripley Odditoriums all around the world. The Ripley archives include the enormous collection that was Robert Ripley's passion.

Always an animal lover, Ripley devoted many cartoons to animal subjects. Naturally, that means the Ripley archives are filled with pieces about animals. Inspired by Ripley's explorations of the animal world, this series of books is designed to give readers a close-up look at the amazing creatures that inhabit Earth.

Some of the most remarkable creatures are among the tiniest—insects. They may be small, but there are lots of them. More than 70 percent of all the animals in the world are insects. And they can do some pretty unbelievable things. Imagine tiny ants that can lift stones fifty times their own body weight. Or cockroaches that can travel five feet in just one second. Then picture the wings of a female mosquito, which can beat 500 times in a second. And there is much, much more to learn—as you are about to find out.

Filled with beautiful photographs, lots of fun facts, and original cartons from the Ripley archives, *Incredible Insects* will amaze you with how extraordinary the tiny creatures known as insects really are.

Prepare to enter the incredible world of insects!

Madeline Boskey, Ph.D.
Series Editor

i

As early as my memories go, I remember having roamed the forests, streams, and fields near my childhood home. I would take things home—salamanders and snakes, plants to press, feathers, owl pellets, the odd rock, or the occasional prize, like the skull of a raccoon. One day when I was about seven years old, I found an insect that was my greatest discovery yet: a wasp with a long abdomen. It had three long, curved, needlelike structures at the tip of its body that curved down and then up over its body, and down again, almost in a circle. A deadly stinger, I thought. The wasp was dutifully pinned with a label, its legs and wings spread, and added to my collection.

At the town library I found a book that helped me identify my alien creature: A species of the genus Megarrhyssa in the huge family of parasitic wasps Ichneumonidae. "The female bores through wood with her long ovipositor to lay eggs into the larvae of wood-boring sawfly larvae," it read. I was hooked. Here was a world alien to the familiar pictures of fighting dinosaurs, field guides, and other natural history lore. In my own backyard there was more natural history walking on six legs than all the birds in North America. Armed with a little microscope my parents gave me that summer, I plunged into my study of insects, wearing a path between the woods and my basement museum and laboratory. The Harvard professor E. O. Wilson said that "every kid goes through a bug phase; some people just never grow out of it." I am one of those people.

Forty years later I'm still at it, with a fascination for insects that continues to grow. It seems odd, but hundreds of scientific papers and newly discovered species haven't jaded me, nor have my travels from the Amazon Basin to the arctic tundra. In fact, the more I learn the more I realize that, besides the ocean, insects are the greatest source of biological discovery and exploration on the planet. There are approximately one million named species, but probably five million species total, meaning that the search to know all species of insects will take many generations. And that's just the basic naming and classifying of them. Understanding their behavior, life histories, and ecology will take far more time but will reveal unimaginable things.

We know, for example, that some species of moths defend themselves by producing the deadly poison cyanide, but how? Many moths are able to hear the high-pitched squeaks of bats with special ears, and they dive-bomb when they hear a bat. But tiger moths send out a high-pitched squeal, which is thought to jam the bat's radar. How does something like that evolve? Even for the basic questions, there are few answers, like: How did wings evolve? The incurable and budding naturalist will take great pleasure in knowing that the depth of discovery in insects is probably bottomless.

I know you will enjoy this book, and I hope that you too will eventually discover your own Megarrhyssa.

Dr. David Grimaldi
Curator, Division of Invertebrate Zoology
American Museum of Natural History

An Ichneumon wasp.

Contents

Incredible Insects 2

Getting Around 7

Sensational Senses 11

It's a Bug Eat Bug World 16

Lifecycles 20

Butterflies and Moths 24

Beetles, Beetles Everywhere 29

Stings and Wings: Bees and Wasps 32

Ants and Termites 38

Flies and Mosquitoes 42

Interacting with Insects 46

Insects Under the Microscope 51

Discover More About Insects 55

Glossary 56

Index 58

Incredible Insects!

The praying mantis gets its name from the way it holds its front legs while waiting for prey. This one is already halfway through lunch!

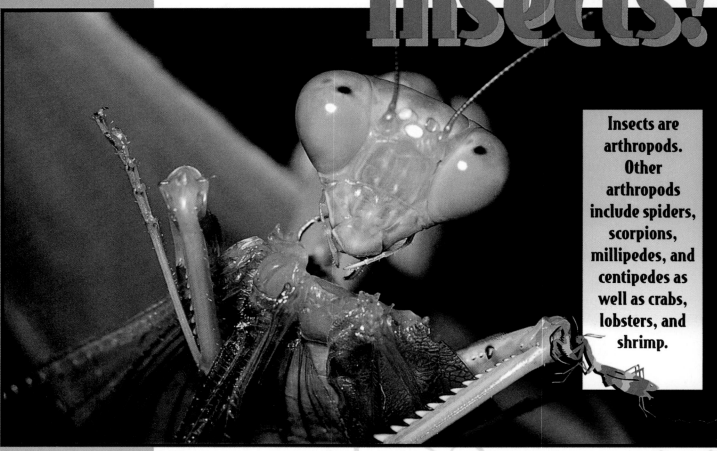

Insects are arthropods. Other arthropods include spiders, scorpions, millipedes, and centipedes as well as crabs, lobsters, and shrimp.

Shown on a barberry flower, the Osmia ribifloris bee is also called the blueberry bee because it pollinates commercial blueberry crops.

Some people get the creeps just hearing the word insect. Others think that insects are totally fascinating. Either way, almost everyone agrees that insects are pretty incredible creatures.

Insects can be real pests. They sometimes bite and sting, destroy crops, and carry diseases. Yet, insects are very necessary for a number of reasons.

Without insects, many plant species would die out altogether. That's because insects pollinate plants, enabling them to reproduce. About 85% of our crops depend on insects to pollinate them.

Animal species are dependent on insects, too. Many animals—including some humans—eat insects. They are a vital food source for many of the world's creatures.

Insects also eat waste products, such as dung, and break down the bodies of dead animals, helping to keep Earth clean. And finally, some insects make products that humans value and use, like honey and silk.

Insects Identified

All insects are members of the animal kingdom. They are invertebrates, which means they have no backbone. More than 75 percent of the animals on Earth are invertebrates.

Insects are arthropods—animals that have exoskeletons. These hard skeletons are on the outside, rather than the inside, of their body.

More than 70 percent of all animals are insects. Entomologists, scientists who study insects, estimate that there are more than five million insect species and only one million are named. And they've only just begun to categorize them. Many entomologists think that a few million more are just waiting to be discovered.

Scientists who study insects are called entomologists.

Dragonflies are fast fliers and incredible hunters. Mosquitoes are just one of the insects they like to dine on.

If you weighed all the insects in the world, they'd weigh more than all the other animals combined. That's a lot of insects!

Some farmers use convergent ladybug beetles to control pests.

Inside Insects

Insects come in a variety of sizes and shapes. There is a dragonfly species in Borneo that has a wingspan of more than 6 inches (15.24 cm). Madagascan giant hissing roaches can grow to be 2 to 3 inches long (5.08 cm to 7.62 cm) and 1 inch (2.54 cm) wide. On the other hand, there are tiny wasps that are smaller than $1/32$ of an inch (.81 mm) long.

Big or small, all insects possess six jointed legs and three main body parts—the head, the thorax, and the abdomen (stomach).

🐜 The head contains the eyes, mouthparts (including mandibles), two antennae, and a simple brain, which is connected to the nervous system.

🐜 Legs and wings are attached to the thorax.

🐜 The abdomen contains most of the digestive system, the heart, and the reproductive organs. The abdomen of some insects may also include "tails," called cerci, which can help insects sense things.

Insects don't breathe like humans do. Instead, they have pores called spiracles on their abdomen and thorax. Air flows into the spiracles and circulate through the body in fine tubes.

Insect species are divided into groups called orders.

Insects have clear or pale yellow or green blood. (The red spot left on the wall when you swatted that mosquito was blood that the bug took in after biting its human or animal victim. Let's hope it wasn't yours, or you're going to start itching right . . . about . . . now!)

Head   Compound eye   Thorax   Wings

Antenna

Mouthparts (mandibles)   Legs   Abdomen

Creepy Crawlers

One way to tell whether a creature is an insect is to count the legs. Adult insects have six legs. Spiders have eight legs. Millipedes and centipedes have hundreds of legs, and worms don't have any. None of these creatures are insects.

Spider

Millipede   Centipede   Worm

"AS STRONG AS GOLIATH" Goliath beetles can carry up to 850 times their own weight.

Weighing up to 3.69 ounces (115 g), the Goliath beetle is the heaviest of all beetles.

Bugging Out

Many people think that the word *bug* means *insect*, but that's not true. Scientifically speaking, all bugs are insects, but not all insects are bugs. Confused? Well, so are lots of people. We tend to use the word bug to refer to any creepy-crawly. But scientists only use the word to refer to a specific order of insects called Hemiptera, or true bugs. In Greek, Hemiptera means "half wings." The bugs originally included in this order had front wings that were partly hardened and partly soft. These "half-wings" gave the true bug order its name. All true bugs have mouthparts that allow them to pierce their food and suck up liquids.

Stinkbugs belong to the true bug, or Hemiptera, order of insects.

Insects Are Old News

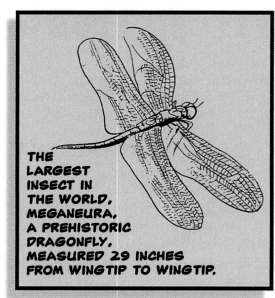

THE LARGEST INSECT IN THE WORLD, MEGANEURA, A PREHISTORIC DRAGONFLY, MEASURED 29 INCHES FROM WINGTIP TO WINGTIP.

There were insects on Earth even before there were dinosaurs. The oldest known insect fossil is about 400 million years old.

Insects are cold-blooded animals. Their body temperature changes depending on how cold or hot it is. Because of this, some insects are able to live through long periods of freezing temperatures. Insects can also reproduce quickly and in great numbers. Their tough exoskeleton helps protect them and conserves body moisture. Their small size gives them an advantage when it comes to hiding and moving quickly. Insects have another edge, too. They can fly. This allows them to avoid predators. It also helps when they want to find food or a mate.

Cockroaches are one of the oldest kinds of insects. Early ancestors of roaches came on the scene more than 300 million years ago. Today, there are 3,500 species of cockroaches throughout the world, with most preferring tropical climates. Only about six species of roaches drive human beings crazy, infesting their homes and eating their food. But those six are enough to give all cockroaches a bad rep.

Animals like dragonflies and cockroaches are sometimes called "living fossils" because they have changed so little since ancient times.

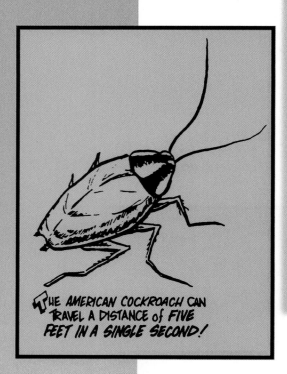

THE AMERICAN COCKROACH CAN TRAVEL A DISTANCE OF *FIVE FEET IN A SINGLE SECOND!*

If you cut off its head, a cockroach will continue to live for a week. At that point, it dies of thirst.

Getting Around

Some insects, like the housefly, have tiny hairs, or bristles, on their feet. They secrete a sticky substance that helps the insect cling to the smoothest of surfaces.

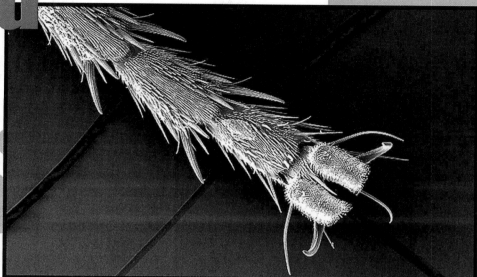

Insects can run, jump, swim, or float, but the most common way they get around is by flying. In fact, insects were the first animals to fly. They were zipping through the air 100 million years before the first pterodactyls (flying reptiles) took flight and nearly 200 million years before the first birds.

Grounded!

In the insect universe, walking closely follows flying as a way to get around. Most insects can walk, and many often do. Cockroaches, for example, have wings but rarely fly. Instead, they use their strong legs to scurry about. Their flat bodies make it easy for them to squeeze into tiny cracks and crevices in case of danger.

You've probably seen insects walk up walls and windows and even on ceilings. So how come they don't fall off? Insect legs have a few nifty features that help their stick-to-itiveness. The last segment of an insect's leg, or its "foot," is called the pretarsus. Pretarsi have little claws that enable insects to grab hold of many different kinds of structures.

Some insects don't bother to travel at all. Lice, for instance, are born, live, and die on their host. Why go anywhere else when you can eat and mate at home?

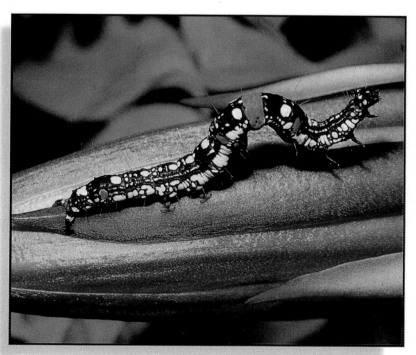

Inchworm caterpillars have a funny, loopy walk. Holding onto the ground with their front legs, they drag their back end forward, scrunching up their middle in a loop. To straighten out, they stretch forward, leaving their back legs in place.

7

Taking Flight

Most adult insects have two pairs of wings. The front pair is usually larger than the back pair. Different insects use their wings in different ways.

Damselflies and dragonflies flap each pair of wings separately when they fly. When dragonflies turn, their front wings actually knock against their back wings, making a clicking sound you can hear if you listen carefully.

Beetles use only their back wings to fly. Their front wings, which are called elytra, are made of a hard material called chiton. When the elytra are folded, they shield both the beetles' rear flying wings and their body. When flying, beetles hold the elytra up out of the way and let their back wings do all the work. Because these back wings aren't very powerful, beetles aren't great fliers. You're more likely to see beetles walking than flying.

Different insects beat their wings at different speeds. Generally, the faster the beat, the faster they travel. The butterfly is one of the slowest insect fliers, beating its wings at only nine to twelve times per second and traveling about 5.5 miles (8.86 km) per hour. Dragonflies may be the fastest insect fliers at 31 miles (150 km) per hour.

Houseflies always take off backward. You can catch a housefly in midair and amaze your friends by just sweeping your hand toward the fly—from behind it. The fly should take off and fly backward directly into your hand! Believe It or Not!

Butterflies may fly slowly, but some of them can go long distances. The painted lady butterfly migrates between Africa and Iceland—a distance of 4,000 miles (6,437 km)!

Monarch butterflies migrate more than 2,000 miles (3,218 km) between Canada and Mexico.

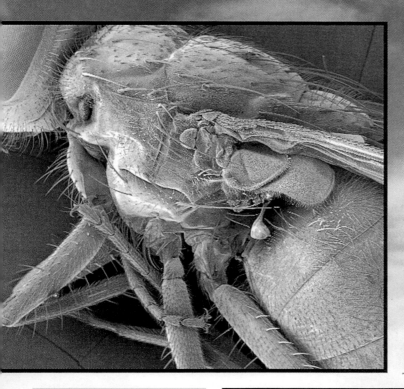

THE COMMON **MIDGE** — A TINY INSECT — BEATS ITS WINGS **133,000 TIMES PER MINUTE!** FLAP FLAP FLAP FLAP FLAP FLAP

The housefly no longer has two pairs of wings. The rear wings evolved into halteres, modified back wings, which stabilize the fly when it's in flight. They help it zip left and right, dart up and down, and even fly backward.

Wasps and bees attach their front and back wings together with hooks when they fly. This makes their wings more powerful and flexible.

Jump!

When it comes to jumping, fleas are the stars of the insect world. To jump as far as a flea, a person would have to jump the length of four football fields! Fleas have special rubbery pads just above each of their large, muscular hind legs. When a flea gets ready to jump, it locks its hind legs against its body, tightly squeezing the pads. When its legs snap free, the pads act like a spring, catapulting the flea high into the air.

Believe It or Not! DRAGONFLIES CAN FLY BACKWARDS!

Grasshoppers can jump up to twenty times their own length. If a person jumped that far, she or he would have to jump the whole length of a basketball court.

Water Ways

There are a variety of ways insects can get around in the water. Some, like the water strider, can walk on the surface. Other insects can swim. Some, such as diving beetles, carry bubbles of air under their wings so they can breathe while swimming underwater. Other insects live underwater and just crawl along the bottoms of streams or ponds. Still others drift along with the current, going wherever the water takes them. Dragonfly nymphs move around by pushing water out of the end of their abdomen, just like a jet engine propels a plane.

Here comes a dytiscid beetle, a predator.

The WHIRLIGIG BEETLE TO ESCAPE ITS SURFACE ENEMIES CRASH DIVES UNDERWATER WITH **A BUBBLE OF AIR TRAPPED BENEATH ITS WING COVERS**

The backswimmer (below) swims upside down in short, jerky movements.

The pull of water molecules from underneath forces molecules on the surface to draw tightly together. This is called surface tension.

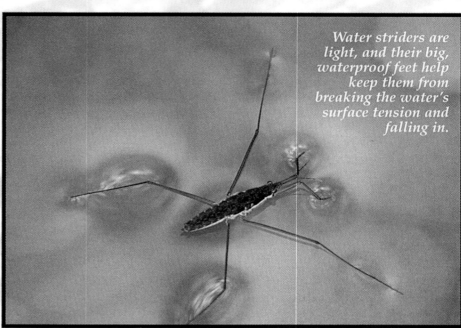

Water striders are light, and their big, waterproof feet help keep them from breaking the water's surface tension and falling in.

Sensational Senses

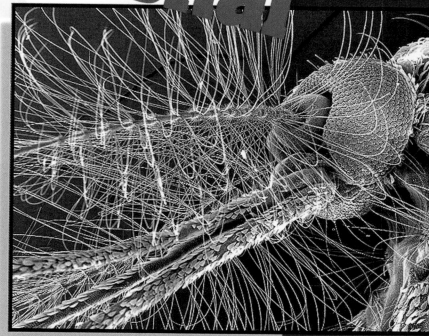

Most insects have the same five senses humans have. They can see, hear, taste, smell, and touch—though not always with the same organs as people or other animals. They use their senses to find food, locate mates, communicate with other insects, and detect danger. Insects may be small, but they can see and hear things humans can't and smell things from miles away.

Insects have microscopic sense organs called sensilla that enable them to detect smells, taste, touch, heat, cold, and in some cases, sound. Most sensilla are found on an insect's antennae, but they can be located almost anywhere on an insect's body.

The male mosquito has much bushier antennae than the female. He uses them to pick up the buzzing sound made by the beating wings of a female of his own species.

How Tasty!

Bees and wasps have taste sensilla on their antennae. But most insects have sensilla for taste located near their mouths. The sensilla have little pores to let in molecules so the insect can tell what it's tasting.

Most insects can taste things that are salty, bitter, sour, and sweet—just like humans.

Like other weevils, the maize weevil uses its mouthparts to bore into its favorite plant, in this case, corn. It uses the clubbed antennae at the end of its mouth to decide whether to lay eggs in the plant or eat it.

Some insects have up to 100,000 sensilla on each antenna!

The Eyes Have It

Insects see in color but more toward the blue end of the spectrum. They can't see red.

Most insects have two kinds of eyes—two compound eyes and up to three simple eyes. Compound eyes are made up of many different facets. Each facet has six sides, and the facets fit together like a honeycomb. Each facet gives a slightly different view of an object that the insect's brain combines into a complete picture. Think of the way we see pictures on a TV screen. TV pictures are made up of bits of light called pixels. The more pixels on the screen, the clearer the picture. The more facets in a compound eye and the more bits of light they take in, the clearer the picture the insect sees.

Compound eyes allow insects to see changes in movement very quickly. No matter how fast something moves, an insect can see it as if it were moving in slow motion. This ability makes it easy for insects to chase other quick-flying insects as well as to fly rapidly from place to place without running into anything.

Some insects' compound eyes have hundreds, sometimes even thousands, of facets. This common fly has its eye on you!

Insects also use their eyes when they're looking for a mate. For example, male fireflies flash light when they're interested in mating. If a female sees the light and wants to get to know the male, she flashes back. The time between flashes tells each insect whether the other is a male or a female.

What people see.

What a bee sees.

THE STALK-EYED FLY HAS EYES THAT STICK OUT SO FAR IT CAN SEE OBJECTS IN FRONT AND BEHIND!

Many insects can see ultraviolet light, which is invisible to humans. When a bee spots a flower that reflects ultraviolet light, it can make a beeline straight for the nectar.

Cockroaches have eyes that let them see in all directions. Imagine! It would be like having eyes in the back of your head!

Simply Seeing

Simple eyes, which are called ocelli, can distinguish between light and dark. The ocelli stimulate the insect to be more or less active depending on how much light there is. This may be what enables insects to know when to hibernate or when to look for food. Ocelli may also help orient an insect and keep it flying level.

A dragonfly's eyes cover most of its head, enabling it to see in all directions—pretty handy when you're looking for lunch. A dragonfly can have up to 30,000 facets in each of its eyes!

13

Sound Effects

Insects also use sensilla to hear. Insects like cicadas, crickets, and moths have more complicated hearing organs, called tympanum, which are similar to human eardrums. Insects can detect sound waves that pass through the air, the ground, water, and even a leaf.

Some insects make noise by rubbing parts of their bodies together. Crickets rub their front wings together. The sharp edge of one wing is rapidly pulled across a series of ridges on the other, making a rasping sound. These sounds can attract female crickets, warn other crickets of danger, or serve as challenges when male crickets are in a fighting mood.

A male cicada uses his strong stomach muscles to vibrate two membranes— like the tops of drums—that are on the sides of his body. This makes a loud, rhythmic noise that can be heard up to a quarter of a mile (.40 km) away. It's sure to attract any female cicadas in the neighborhood—and drive you crazy on hot summer days!

KATYDIDS HEAR THROUGH SLITS IN THEIR LEGS!

Ants communicate by touching antennae. This allows them to pass along chemical messages to one another.

Touchy-Feely

Touch sensilla are usually hairs with tiny nerve endings at their base. When the hair is moved in any way, even by the gentlest of breezes, the insect can sense it. Fine hairs on the cerci of roaches are so sensitive that they have a direct connection to the legs—not to the brain. That makes for a really quick getaway!

14

Scent of a Female

Female insects often produce "smelly" chemicals called pheromones to attract mates, and male insects can detect a tiny amount of these scents, often at great distances. A male silk moth can smell the pheromones of a female moth that's more than 2 miles (3.22 km) away!

Smell Is Swell

Insects have a keen sense of smell—far keener than a human's. They detect odors through sensilla, which are located mostly on their antennae. Like taste sensilla, the sensilla that pick up odors have at least one small hole, or pore, in each one.

Many insects find food by scent. Some insects that feed on animals, such as the mosquito, can even detect the carbon dioxide breathed out by other animals and follow it to find the source of their next meal (which could be you!). Insects also use scent to communicate. For example, ants can lay a scented trail to lead other ants to any tasty treats they happen to find.

If a female silkworm moth sprayed all the pheromones in her sac at once, she'd attract a trillion male moths in seconds. Talk about attraction!

A smell emitted by a queen bee discourages other bees from laying eggs and encourages them to go out and look for food.

A BEE HAS 5,000 TASTE BUDS AND CAN SMELL AN APPLE TREE LOCATED THREE MILES AWAY!

Ants use their antennae to pick up the scent of food.

15

It's a Bug EAT Bug World

I nsects have many enemies, including other insects. What does an insect do if it senses danger nearby? Its first line of defense is to run—or jump or fly—away.

Some insects are poisonous to eat, painful to touch, or unpleasant to smell. These insects often have special colors or patterns that act as warning signs to predators. Assassin bugs, which have a nasty bite, have two bright spots on their back that give the message, "Stay away." Monarch butterflies are brightly colored to warn birds of their nasty taste.

Other insects stink—literally. Leaf-footed bugs and stinkbugs secrete smelly chemicals to discourage predators from eating them. Shield bugs emit a chemical that can make predators, including people, feel sick for days. Some insects actively defend themselves by stinging or biting. A New Guinea walking stick has sharp spines that it uses to stab its enemies.

Spiny oak slug moth caterpillars have up to 50 stinging spines. Ouch!

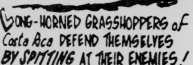

PTUI
LONG-HORNED GRASSHOPPERS of Costa Rica DEFEND THEMSELVES BY SPITTING AT THEIR ENEMIES!

When it spreads its wings, the eye spots on a polyphemus moth may startle a predator.

Hiding in Plain Sight

Many insects are protected from predators by camouflage. That's when an insect evolves to look like something in its environment, such as a leaf or a stick. Green leaves, dead leaves, thorns, twigs, tree bark, rotted wood, bird droppings—there are insects that look like all of these things. An insect using camouflage to protect itself must stay completely still to avoid ending up as a tasty snack.

Bright green katydids look a lot like green leaves.

Stick insects look exactly like their namesake. Some of them even sway like a twig in the breeze when danger is near.

Fooled You!

Mimicry is when an insect has evolved to look like another insect, animal, or even object—a less tasty or a more dangerous one. One hawk moth caterpillar, for example, looks like a small snake. A hornet clearwing moth looks exactly like a hornet—a kind of wasp. Any creature that's been stung by a hornet will certainly avoid this moth.

Some insects have protective coloration. Moth species like the Io moth have big, bright eyespots of color on their wings that aren't visible when the wings are closed. But when they open, the spots flash like giant eyes, surprising the predator and allowing the moth to escape.

THE OWL BUTTERFLY IS NOT HARMED BY PREDATORS BECAUSE ITS CAMOUFLAGE MAKES IT LOOK LIKE A *FIERCE BIRD OF PREY*

Really Bad Taste

Monarch butterflies have a bright orange and black body. You'd think birds would pick them off like ripe berries, but they don't. That's because monarchs eat milkweed, which makes them taste terrible. Scientists once thought the viceroy butterfly mimicked the monarch to fool birds, but they now know that viceroys also taste bad. Any bird that's had a mouthful of either one will probably avoid all orange and black butterflies for the rest of its life.

Most insect predators digest their food by injecting a chemical that turns the prey's insides to mush. Then the predators slurp them up.

Mantises are amazing examples of predators that use camouflage. You may have been surprised by a praying mantis that looked a lot like the plant it was sitting on. But there are also some that look like orchids, fungus, and bird droppings.

Gotcha!

Insect hunters are as clever as their prey. About one-third of all insects are carnivorous, that is, they eat meat. Ants are the most important carnivores on Earth. If they didn't eat the insects they do, the planet would soon be overrun. A large colony of wood ants is capable of devouring thousands of other insects—like caterpillars—in just one day.

Insects catch other insects by being faster, seeing better or more quickly, or using weapons. They may have powerful jaws or stingers that grab or immobilize their prey. Some predators even use camouflage to surprise their unwitting prey.

A parasitic wasp prepares to lay an egg in an immature tarnished plant bug.

Young and Dangerous

Some phorid flies are natural enemies of ants, including fire ants. The female phorid pierces the ant's head, lays an egg, and the growing larva will later make its head fall off!

Parasites live on or in the bodies of their hosts and survive by eating them—in some cases, from the inside out. Certain species of wasps, for example, sniff out grasshopper eggs, then lay their own eggs inside. When the wasp eggs hatch, the wasp larvae feed on the grasshopper eggs.

The female cicada killer wasp paralyzes a cicada by stinging it. She then drags the still-living cicada back to her nest. Each nest has many cells. The wasp puts one or two cicadas in each cell. Then she lays a single egg in each cell. When the egg hatches, the wasp larva eats the cicada (or cicadas) in the cell.

Other wasps lay their eggs inside the body of caterpillars, beetle grubs (the beetle larvae), and even tarantulas.

Some insect parasites prey on humans. Head lice lay eggs on human hair. When they hatch, their mouthparts allow them to pierce the scalp and suck up blood.

Fire ants grab their prey with their jaws and sting it repeatedly.

19

Lifecycles

Just about all insects lay eggs. Some insects don't need to mate in order to lay eggs that can hatch. Female aphids, for instance, can give birth without mating, but only to other females. In order to produce male aphids, they need to mate.

Most insects need to mate to produce offspring. How does an insect go about finding a mate? To start out, it would have to identify a mate from its own species, or at least one that's similar enough so that it can mate successfully. This isn't as easy as you might think.

To attract females, male butterflies do special "dancing flights" that are unique to each species.

Female glowworms flash a special light near the ends of their abdomens to attract male glowworms. Some even flash in code!

Mating Rituals

Some insects use their sense of smell to find a mate. Others use sight. Some males visit feeding sites or even particular plants that females of their species like. Male bees swarm in a mating dance that attracts queens. Some male insects woo females with gifts.

Once an insect has found an appropriate mate, reproduction begins. Male insects carry sperm in their bodies, and female insects carry eggs. When they mate, the male insect propels sperm into the female's body. The sperm goes to a kind of holding area where she stores it. When the female lays her eggs, they are fertilized by the sperm as they leave her body.

Some species of dance flies actually bring gifts to their potential mates. Sometimes, the package is full of insect prey. Sometimes, the dance fly males fool the females, and their gift boxes are empty.

Believe It or Not! WHEN PURSUING A FEMALE, A MALE DRAGONFLY CAN REACH SPEEDS of 87 MPH!

A single female Mexican fruit fly can lay up to 40 eggs at a time, 100 or more a day, and about 2,000 over her life span!

Some female aphids start out as eggs, and others are born live. All males, however, start out as eggs.

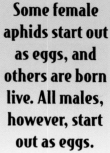

A Colorado potato beetle larva is just hatching from its egg.

Eggs-tra Protection

Though most female insects lay their eggs and take off, some females will guard their eggs. For instance, go too near a stinkbug's eggs or young and you'll find out why she's called a stinkbug! Male insects very rarely take care of eggs, but some male assassin bugs are exceptions. They will defend the eggs of their mates.

Most insects make sure that there is a plentiful supply of food nearby so that when the eggs hatch, the young have enough to eat. The female insects of many species lay their eggs right inside the food.

Shield bug mothers will stand over their eggs (and their young) and try to scare off any predators looking for a meal.

Marvels of Metamorphosis

The incredible process by which an egg becomes an adult insect is called metamorphosis. There are two kinds of metamorphosis—incomplete, or simple, and complete. Some insects, such as springtails, silverfish, dragonflies, damselflies, grasshoppers, crickets, cockroaches, walking sticks, and mantises, go through simple metamorphosis. Other insects, including butterflies, moths, beetles, mosquitoes, flies, fleas, ants, wasps, and bees, go through complete metamorphosis.

Damselfly nymphs live underwater and breathe through gills at the end of their abdomens.

Simply Growing Up

In simple metamorphosis, the tiny insect that hatches from an egg is called a nymph. Most nymphs look a lot like miniature adults, but they still have to develop wings and reproductive organs. Some nymphs don't look anything at all like they will as adults. Some of these, such as damselfly and dragonfly nymphs, even live underwater until their final molt.

As a nymph grows and changes, it molts. All arthropods molt because their exoskeletons don't grow. When an exoskeleton "suit" gets tight, the arthropod splits it open and struggles out of it. Underneath is a soft, new, bigger exoskeleton that will soon harden. Insects usually have to molt at least three times before they can grow into adults.

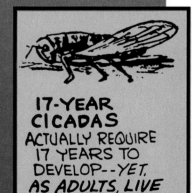

17-YEAR CICADAS ACTUALLY REQUIRE 17 YEARS TO DEVELOP--YET, AS ADULTS, LIVE ONLY 30 TO 40 DAYS

It can take anywhere from an hour to several days for an insect, such as a cicada, to molt.

The larva of a green lacewing dines on whitefly nymphs.

The female screwworm lays her eggs in living animals. When the larvae hatch, their tusklike mandibles rasp the flesh, causing wounds that may get infected. Other females lay their eggs in infected wounds. An animal that becomes infested with screwworm larvae can die.

Going Through a Stage

Complete metamorphosis is an even more amazing process. During complete metamorphosis, the insect changes its form—both inside and out—all at once instead of little by little. The young insect that hatches from the egg is called a larva, and it's always totally different from its parents. Larvae often look kind of squishy and wormy. The larvae of butterflies and moths, for example, are caterpillars. Beetle larvae are called grubs, and certain fly larvae are called maggots.

Larvae eat (and eat and eat), grow, and molt until they're ready to pupate, or develop into an adult insect. An insect in this stage is called a pupa. The word pupa also refers to the structure that many insects build to protect them as they develop from larvae into adults. The caterpillar, for example, builds a cocoon. During this stage, the pupa's structure and internal organs change. It also grows some new organs, including wings and reproductive organs. When it's finished doing all this work, it breaks out of its case by using its legs or jaws, or simply by swelling parts of its body. Then there it is: a grown-up insect.

23

Butterflies and Moths

Moths and butterflies belong to the order Lepidoptera. There are 165,000 species of moths and butterflies. These range from less than a quarter of an inch (.63 cm) in size to about 12 inches (30.50 cm) from wingtip to wingtip. They live all over the world. Most have fairly short life spans once they're full grown, usually living no longer than a week or so. Some, however, hibernate through the winter. Monarch butterflies that hatch in the fall migrate. They fly south in the winter and back north in the summer. They can live to be eight or nine months old.

Unlike most moths, the cecropia moth is as colorful as its butterfly relatives. With a wingspan of 4 to 6 inches (10.16 to 15.24 cm), it is the largest moth in North America.

The great spangled fritillary butterfly can be found throughout much of the United States and in southwestern Canada.

The Kamehameha is the official state butterfly of Hawaii. Note its clubbed antennae.

Amazing Transformations

Moths and butterflies both undergo complete metamorphosis. They begin their lives as eggs that hatch into caterpillar larvae. These caterpillars eat and eat and eat, mostly leaves, to build up their strength for what lies ahead. Then they either burrow underground, where they change in little silk-lined cells, create chrysalid or cocoons, or simply attach themselves to a source of food. That's when the hard work begins—transforming from a fat little caterpillar into a butterfly or a moth. When the full-grown adult emerges from its hiding place, its wings expand and harden. At last it's ready to fly.

The mourning cloak butterfly is shown in three stages: caterpillar, chrysalis, and adult.

Getting a Leg Up

Caterpillars have the usual six legs attached to their thoraxes, but they also have a number of "prolegs" attached to their abdomens. The prolegs have tiny hooks on them that enable the caterpillars to grab onto the plants they like to eat. Slugmoth caterpillars have suckers instead of prolegs, giving them a gliding motion—hence their name.

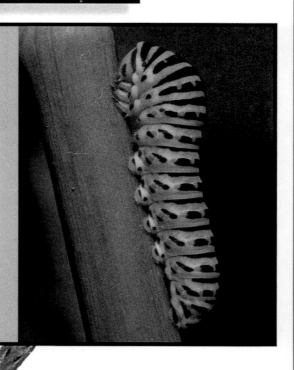

Like all winged insects, butterfly and moth wings have a system of tubes in them. When the insects emerge from their cocoons, air and blood get pumped into the veins so that their wrinkled wings can expand and smooth out.

25

Beautiful Butterflies

Most people think butterflies are among nature's most beautiful creatures. In addition to looking good, butterflies don't bite or hurt humans in any way. They hang out around flowers a good deal of the time. And they change from creepy-crawly little caterpillars into colorful winged creatures—a classic ugly duckling story. No wonder people like them!

Butterflies have four delicate wings that are covered in tiny overlapping scales. These scales form the dusty coating that rubs off on your hands if you touch a butterfly.

Butterfly antennae are segmented, and end in little swellings or knobs known as clubs. They have a long tube called a proboscis, which they use to suck up nectar and other liquids, such as tree sap, decaying fruit and animal juices, and even urine.

When butterflies are not eating, their long proboscis is coiled up.

The Lange's metalmark butterfly gets its name from the metallic-looking spots and lines on its wings.

Swallowtail butterflies get their names from the narrow "tail" at the end of their hind wings.

Conservationists are making efforts to save the jewel-like Karner blue butterfly, which has been listed as an endangered species since 1992.

Mostly Moths

There are many more moths than butterflies. More than 95 percent of Lepidoptera are moths. Most people don't have the same affection for moths, however, even though there is no real scientific difference between them and their butterfly relatives. Like butterflies, moths have four wings covered with tiny scales as well as segmented antennae. In fact, butterflies are just day-flying, fancy moths!

Not all moths have proboscides. Instead, some have short mouthparts that stab into food, while others have no mouthparts at all. They live off their own body fat, built up when they were larvae. For the most part, moths don't bite or hurt humans, either.

Of course, both moth and butterfly larvae can be very destructive to plants and food crops. Some can be real garden pests or even threaten whole species of plants or trees. Cabbage butterfly caterpillars, for example, eat many plants in the mustard family. Gypsy moth caterpillars feed primarily on oak and aspen trees. Moths may also lay their eggs in your sweater drawer so their larvae can eat the wool.

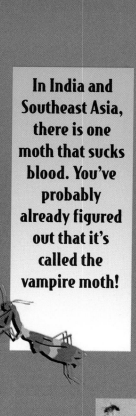

A HAWK *MOTH OF MADAGASCAR* HAS A 12-INCH-LONG *TONGUE!*

The beautiful luna moth is rarely seen because it lives in forests and comes out only at night. Its wingspan can be as much as 4 inches (10.16 cm).

In India and Southeast Asia, there is one moth that sucks blood. You've probably already figured out that it's called the vampire moth!

Very Eary

Many moths actually have ears! They are tuned to the frequencies of bat noise, which helps the moths avoid becoming bat food! Some moths can also make sounds that will discourage bats from chasing and eating them.

Every so often, millions of gypsy moth caterpillars appear, eating the leaves of every tree in sight. The Aleoides indiscretus wasp is a natural enemy of the caterpillar, laying its eggs inside the caterpillar's body. When the eggs hatch, the larvae will eat the caterpillar from the inside out!

Butterfly or Moth?

Most moths are less colorful than butterflies. They can also be a little fuzzy or furry. When they rest, butterflies tend to hold their wings vertical to their bodies—that is, standing straight up. Moths rest with their wings flat and pulled in more closely into their bodies. Moths' antennae are usually feathery looking or threadlike and rarely end in clubs like those of butterflies.

Another difference is that most butterflies are active during the day, while most moths are active at night or at dawn or dusk. This may be why moths use their sense of smell to find mates, while butterflies primarily use sight.

A Parnassian butterfly feeding from a Columbine flower.

The fuzzy body and segmented antennae are clearly visible on this moth.

The larva of this plain-looking moth is a crop pest called the sugarcane borer.

Beetles, Beetles Everywhere

You're probably familiar with a number of beetles already—think of the ladybug and the firefly—but you're certain to see many, many more of these incredible insects in your lifetime. One-third of all the known insects on Earth are beetles, of the order Coleoptera.

Ladybugs are some of the most familiar beetles. Their shiny, spotted bodies are easily recognizable.

There are about 350,000 species of beetles currently known, the largest number of species not only in the insect world, but also in the entire animal kingdom.

Beetle Bodies

What distinguishes beetles from other insects is that they don't use their front wings for flying. These wings, which are called elytra, are strong and hard. When the beetle is not flying, the elytra cover and protect the delicate back wings, usually meeting in a neat seam down the center of the beetle's back. Elytra are often brightly colored and give beetles their smooth, hard, and often shiny appearance. Beetles also have a thicker, tougher exoskeleton than other insects. Given the extra weight and only one pair of flying wings, beetles are not powerful fliers. Most only fly to get from one food source to another.

Beetles have relatively flat, compact bodies that can fit into small hiding places. Their segmented antennae can be clubbed or threadlike. All beetles go through complete metamorphosis.

In the summer, fireflies hide out in the daytime. At dusk, they come out and flash their lights to attract mates.

The click beetle tries to escape notice by lying on its back and playing dead. But if it's attacked, it snaps a joint between the thorax and abdomen up—click!—to flip itself into the air and away from danger.

29

What's for Dinner?

A fast runner and fierce predator, a metallic green tiger beetle uses its powerful jaws to grab prey.

Beetles and their larvae eat all kinds of things, from animals (both dead and alive) to plant material to animal dung. Meat-eating beetles have well-developed mouthparts that can easily crush, chew, and swallow other insects or insect larvae. Many beetle larvae have biting mouthparts, too.

Diving beetles live in streams, lakes, and other bodies of freshwater. They stay underwater for long periods of time by breathing bubbles of air that they trap under their elytra. Large diving beetles will even attack tadpoles and small fish—as will their larvae, which are so fierce they're called water tigers!

Stag beetles, named for the large, antlerlike jaws of the male of the species, may look fierce, but they eat only plant material or honeydew, a waste product of aphids. Tumblebugs, also called dung beetles, use their legs to roll bits of dung into balls. The females lay their eggs inside. When the larvae hatch, they have to eat their way out. They actually feed on the dung.

Japanese beetles have been eating American crops ever since they were discovered in New Jersey in 1916. They probably arrived in the roots of iris plants that a nursery imported from Japan.

Beetle Bad Guys

Many beetles and their larvae are extremely destructive to plants. Goldsmith beetles can strip a cottonwood tree of its leaves in a night. Click beetle larvae, which are called wireworms, often damage food and cotton crops by eating the roots and seeds. The Eastern spotted cucumber beetle is extremely destructive, damaging all kinds of crops, from cucumbers to peanuts.

The larvae of flour beetles, called mealworms, might show up in your breakfast cereal. They eat flour, oatmeal, and other grains. Though death-watch beetles feed on oak trees, they're just as likely to eat your precious antique furniture.

Cotton farmers hate the boll weevil with good reason. The adult boll weevil eats the flower buds and bolls (seedpods), while its larvae live and eat inside the bolls.

The Aphthona flava flea beetle has been imported into the United States to help control leafy spurge, a Eurasian plant that has displaced native grasses across the Great Plains since being introduced in the 19th century.

The European red-bellied clerid beetle dines on pine shoot beetles, which are destructive to pine trees.

Beetle Heroes

Other beetles are heroes of the insect world. Many beetles are pollinators. Others eat dung, helping to clean up the Earth. Some bury dung for their larvae to eat. But they bury so much more than their offspring need that they actually help fertilize plants and enrich the soil.

Some beetles eat insect pests. Downy leather-wings and a variety of ladybug species feed on aphids and other pests. One ladybug species, the vedalia beetle, helped reduce the destruction of citrus orchards in California by the cottony cushion scale, an insect that had accidentally been imported from Australia. Carabid beetles eat harmful caterpillars, such as the gypsy moth and budworm caterpillars, while firefly larvae eat slugs and snails, which can damage crops.

In ancient Egypt, scarabs—stone, glazed clay, and jeweled models of scarab beetles—were used as ornaments or jewelry.

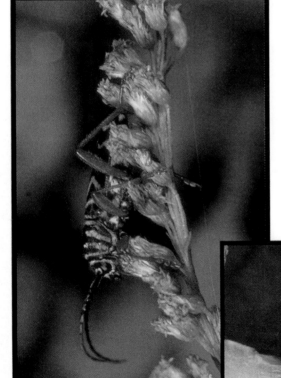

The locust borer (above) feasts on goldenrod pollen and nectar. Its larvae eat the sapwood of black locust trees.

In addition to helping itself to potatoes, the Colorado potato leaves beetle eats other crops, such as tomatoes, eggplants, and peppers.

STINGS AND WINGS: BEES AND WASPS

Bees, wasps, and ants belong to Hymenoptera, one of the largest orders of insects in the world. There are about 120,000 species of Hymenoptera identified at the present time. All Hymenoptera have sections of abdomen that are constricted, creating a slender "waist." All undergo complete metamorphosis.

Most insects are loners. They may mate and have offspring, but other than that, it's every insect for himself or herself. But Hymenoptera are different. Some lead very social lives. Many bees and wasps live in complex societies in which there are rulers, slaves, workers, and soldiers. They have a common purpose: to protect one another and jointly raise their young.

Hymenoptera are also among the most beneficial of insects. Bees pollinate flowers and help a variety of crops to grow. Wasps eat insects like caterpillars, keeping pesky insect populations down. We think of bees and wasps primarily in terms of their stingers. But without bees and wasps, insect pests would destroy most crops we depend on.

A blue orchard bee doing its job, pollinating a zinnia.

This sweat bee is collecting nectar and pollen from a dandelion. Actually, only a few species of sweat bees are attracted to sweat. So don't sweat it!

This joe-pye weed has attracted a fat, furry bumblebee.

A wasp gets ready to lay an egg in the pupal tunnel of a corn earworm.

Honey, We're Home

Honeybees are the most famous of all bees. That's because of the delicious honey they make from flower nectar. When water evaporates from the nectar, it thickens into honey. This honey serves as a nutritious bee food when flowers and nectar aren't available.

Honeybees make their honey where they live—in hives. Hives can house up to 20,000 bees. A hive consists of a group of wax cells called honeycomb. Each cell is six sided and has two ends.

Honeycomb cells are used for two purposes. In the brood comb, or nursery area of the hive, the queen lays her eggs in cells, which are then used to house young honeybees as they're raised. Honey and pollen are stored in other cells.

People long ago learned how to keep bees and harvest honey for themselves. Modern hives have frames in which the six-sided combs sit. These frames can easily be pulled out and drained of honey. Beekeepers usually wear special suits, however, in case any of the worker bees object.

Honeycombs are so perfectly made, it's hard to believe that bees don't use rulers! (Oops, they do... their queens!)

Not all bees live in hives. Carpenter bees, as you might guess from their name, bore into wood, where the females lay their eggs. Male carpenter bees may look like they're about to attack you if you get too close, but they have no stingers. And the females rarely sting. The only problem is that the carpenter bee looks an awful lot like a bumblebee. You might not want to get close enough to tell the difference!

Beehive Bee-havior

The head of a hive is the queen bee. Queen bees are the only bees that mate and lay fertilized eggs. Most of the queen's female offspring become sterile worker bees. Worker bees do everything it takes to keep a hive going. House bees work at home, tending the young and the queen, cleaning, constructing combs, and defending the hive. Older workers become field bees. These are the bees that go out to forage for flowers and their nectar and pollen, which are both used as food by the bees. Field bees have special pollen baskets on each hind leg, and each has an extra stomach for carrying nectar or honey back to the hive. They also gather water and materials needed to construct the hive.

A queen bee can lay up to 1,500 eggs a day and will live two to eight years. That's a lot of baby bees!

Don't worry. This swarm of honeybees isn't interested in you. They have a queen to serve!

Life as a Bee

Male offspring of queen bees are called drones. The drones' only job is to fertilize any new queens that are born. Only a few hundred or so drones live in a hive at any time. At the end of a season, drones that are still alive are driven out of the hive to die.

A few very special female larvae, fed on special royal jelly, become new queens. But only one new queen will survive per hive. The first queen that is born will kill all the other queens as they hatch. Her queen mother, in the meantime, leaves the hive before her bloodthirsty daughter hatches, along with a swarm of workers. Together, they will found a new bee colony.

After dispensing with her royal sisters, the new queen bee will go on a mating flight. During this flight, she may mate with 18 or more drones. Each of the drones will die. The new queen will then start laying eggs, which will be her job for the rest of her life.

The mustached mud bee uses his mustache to woo female bees.

This field bee will head back to her hive once her pollen baskets are full.

Shall Bee Dance?

Worker bees tell each other where to find flowers with nectar in them by dancing. Three bee dances have been identified. The first is called the round dance. Bees dance the round when there are supplies of pollen or nectar within 80 feet (24.38 m) of their hive. Then there's the waggle dance. Bees waggle when there's food that's farther than 320 feet (97.54 m) from the hive. The number of waggles tells other bees how far away the food is and how much of it there is. The angle of the waggles tells the direction of the food relative to the sun. The last bee dance is the vibration dance. In this dance, worker bees in contact with other bees vibrate their abdomens. This dance gathers bees together to forage for food.

Bees' wings beat at about 200 beats per second. That's what makes the bees buzz.

Bee Afraid. Bee Very Afraid.

The honeybee's bright yellow and black stripes are no accident. Their color warns predators that the bees can and will defend themselves. Bees do this by using their stingers. Only female bees can sting, however. Male bees don't have stingers.

Most bee stingers have barbs in them. When a bee stings you, she can't withdraw the stinger because the barb gets stuck. So she tears off her stinger when she flies away. Her injuries later kill her. Only a queen bee's stinger has no barbs on it. She can sting again and again.

A **BEE** USES **22** DIFFERENT MUSCLES TO STING SOMEONE!

35

The Wonderful World of Wasps

While bees make up for their stingers by providing us with honey, wasps are less obviously useful. In fact, most humans are just plain nervous around wasps. But wasps actually do a heroic job of keeping insect populations down and our food plants thriving. Without wasps, Earth would be much poorer place, and we would have less to eat.

Many wasps are solitary creatures. They catch other insects, paralyze them, and lay their eggs nearby—sometimes very nearby—so their larvae can feed as it grows.

Tiphid wasps, for example, paralyze beetle larvae with their stingers and then lay an egg on each larva's body. Digger wasps sting and paralyze an insect or spider and then bury it along with one of their eggs. Jewel wasps actually invade the nests of other solitary wasp or bee larvae and lay their own eggs there. The jewel wasp larva then eats the host larva and all of its food stores.

Because they eat insects, social wasps don't store food in their nests. That's because there's no such thing as a wasp refrigerator—so the meat would soon go bad.

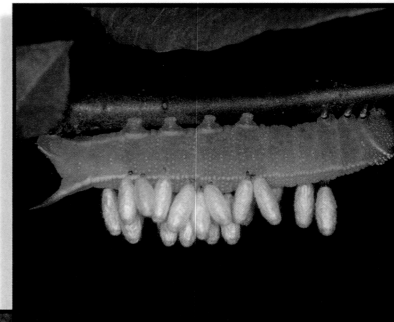

Yikes! This sphinx moth caterpillar is being parasitized by some braconid wasp larvae.

Home sweet home to yellow jacket hornets.

36

Paper wasps chew on trees, wood buildings, fences, even paper or cardboard. They chew the wood or paper fibers they've collected, which mix with their saliva. After the fibers get soft, the wasp spreads the material on her nest using her legs and mouthparts. It dries into a long-lasting, durable paper.

The Ways of Wasps

THE **PAPER NEST** of some Brazilian wasps *LOOKS LIKE A JAPANESE LANTERN— ACTUALLY IT IS A MINIATURE SKYSCRAPER, COMPRISING 20 OR MORE STORIES*

Social wasps, on the other hand—like paper wasps, yellow jackets, hornets, and mason wasps—live together in nests made from chewed wood (or, in the case of the mason wasp, mud-lined underground nests). They have queens and workers, just like honeybees. Social wasp communities are known as colonies. A paper wasp colony might be found attached to a tree or a building and contain from 15 to 200 wasps. Yellow jacket colonies tend to be underground or in spaces between the walls of buildings and can contain 5,000 or more insects. These yellow jackets will sting repeatedly if someone disturbs their nest.

Wasps' stingers are made from modified egg-laying tubes, so males do not have stingers. After a wasp punctures her victim with her sharp stinger, wasp venom is pumped out through the stinger and into the wound. The barbs on the end of wasps' stingers are small, and wasps can easily pull their stingers out after attacking a victim. This means wasps can sting again and again.

Wasp communities usually die out after one season, and old nests are never used again. Young queens who are fertilized by drones may hibernate over the winter and start their own colonies the next spring.

The largest wasp nest on record measured 12 feet (3.66 m) long with a diameter of 5 feet 9 inches (1.75 m). It was discovered on a farm in New Zealand in 1963.

How do you think the yellow jacket got its name?

Hornets (larger members of the wasp family) live in a nest like this one.

Ants and Termites

All About Ants

Ants often build nests in wood.

Another social insect from the order Hymenoptera is the ant. Ten thousand species of ants have been categorized. Many more live in rain forests that are being destroyed and will probably die out before they're ever discovered.

Although ants can be pests, they are very important. That's because ants are the cleaners of the Earth. More animal matter is consumed by ants than by all other carnivorous animals combined.

Another ant is probably not far behind. Ants are very social creatures.

Ants' Antics

Ants live in colonies that can contain up to several million individuals. These colonies are headed by fertilized, winged queens. The colonies also include worker ants and male ants. Workers are wingless, infertile sisters who take care of their larval sisters, find food, and defend the nest. Male ants, like drones, usually have wings, so that they can catch and mate with the queen. Then they die. Queens lose their wings after they mate. The rest of their lives are spent laying eggs.

FLEX FLEX

ANTS CAN LIFT *STONES* THAT WEIGH 50 TIMES THEIR OWN WEIGHT—EQUAL TO A MAN CARRYING A 4-TON CAR UP A HILL!

South American army ants live in huge colonies of up to one million!

Ants at Home

Ants protect themselves by biting, stinging, or producing formic acid. Formic acid can also be found in many plants.

Most ants build nests in which to live. Some of these nests are dug out of the ground. Ants use their mouthparts to do this. They smooth out dirt corridors using their saliva. Other ants live in structures that are both underground and above ground. Some ants build nests inside tree trunks and branches, hollowing out spaces by chewing up new wood. Others weave leaves together to form nests, using a kind of silk from the glands of their larvae to hold the leaves together.

Ant nests may look a little disorganized, but for the most part, they're models of efficiency. Eggs, larvae, and pupae are moved around the nest, depending on the temperature needed to sustain them. There are ventilation shafts that can be opened or closed if the ants want air. When it's too warm, the ants move to the lower levels of their nest. When it gets cold, they move up to take advantage of the warmth of the sun.

Army ants, the greatest hunters in the ant kingdom, don't actually build nests. There's no point—they won't stick around long enough in any one place to need them. Instead, they live in nests formed of live ant bodies. When they get hungry, these ants spread out and kill anything that can't get out of their way, including spiders, small birds, lizards, and other animals. Then they go into their stationary stage, and the queen lays all her eggs. When these eggs have developed into larvae and the ants need food again, they become nomadic once more.

MANY TYPES OF DESERT ANTS CARRY THEIR DEAD TO ANT CEMETERIES

The leaf-cutting ants that find and collect fresh leaves are always the next-to-smallest workers in their ant colony. Other workers are busy building the nest, raising fungus, and guarding the nest.

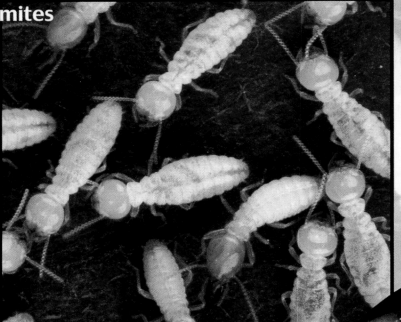

Totally Termite

People sometimes confuse termites with ants because they can look quite similar. But termites actually belong to a completely different order of insect, Isoptera. All termites eat wood, and all live in communities not unlike those of ants, bees, and wasps. There are two basic types of termites—those that burrow into wood, and those that live in the ground.

When Formosan subterranean termites are fed red-stained filter paper, they turn red and scientists can track their movements.

Scientists have determined that a group of 20-foot-high (6.09 m) sandstone pillars found near Gallup, New Mexico, are probably giant fossils of termite nests that are about 155 million years old. Some of these fossil nests also reach 120 feet (36.58 m) below the ground!

Wood-Burrowing Ways

Wood-burrowing termites live in dead trees or logs or other wood structures. Once the dead wood is eaten, the colony dies. These termites undergo incomplete metamorphosis. The nymphs of these termites act as workers, staying in the nests to help the adults raise more termites. Others act as guards against the termite's worst enemy—the ant. Most nymphs eventually grow wings and fly away to start their own colonies.

Most termites are the kind that burrow into the ground. This doesn't mean they don't eat wood—they do. It just means that they're capable of finding many different pieces of dead plants to eat as they dig around. (Many termites eat dried grasses, or even dried dung.) It also means that their colonies can grow much larger than their wood-burrowing cousins, who disappear when their source of food runs out. Thousands to millions of termites can be part of a ground-dwelling termite colony.

These Formosan subterranean termite workers and soldiers are repairing a hole in their nest.

Believe It or Not! A QUEEN TERMITE CAN LIVE for UP TO 20 YEARS!

Formosan termite alates live only to reproduce.

Termites in Africa and Australia can build remarkably large mounds. African mound termites, for example, are able to build mounds over a number of years that are over 18 feet (5.5 m) tall. But the nest itself is actually below ground. Up to two million termites may live in each nest.

Life Underground

Subterranean (underground) termite colonies consist of both reproductive and worker termites. The reproductive termites, called alates or swarmers, are both male and female. Alates only exist to reproduce. They go on one short flight, then shed their wings and go looking for a mate. These wingless alates become the kings and queens of new termite nests. Termite queens can lay up to 30,000 eggs a day. They're so fat that they can't move, so workers carry their eggs away to chambers to be reared.

Worker termites care for the young termites, build nests, forage for food, and build mud tubes and tunnels. Soldier termites defend the colony. These may have large heads and jaws that snap, chew, or do other nasty things to intruders. They may also secrete chemicals that serve as weapons against their enemies.

Though all termites eat dried plant matter and some can destroy homes and trees, most termite species are still considered beneficial insects, for in the process of digesting wood, they add it to the ground, enriching and aerating the soil and providing food and homes for other insect species.

Tele-Termite

Termites communicate by secreting pheromones. Each colony of termites has a particular smell, and termite soldiers recognize an intruder by its different odor. An alarm pheromone is then secreted, and the soldiers attack. When a worker termite finds a new food source, it can lay a chemical trail for other termites to follow. The number of workers, soldiers, or reproductive termites is also regulated by smell.

Termites communicate by sound, too. Soldiers and workers sometimes bang their heads against the tunnel walls, creating vibrations that can be heard by other termites, who rush to defend the colony.

This huge mound was built by industrious termites!

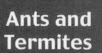

Flies and Mosquitoes

The name "mosquito" is the Spanish word for "little fly."

Perhaps the least popular insects of all are mosquitoes and other flies. Nobody seems to have a nice word to say about them. They spread diseases like malaria, encephalitis, yellow fever, West Nile virus, and sleeping sickness. (Malaria alone has killed more people throughout history than any other known disease. It still kills about a million people a year.) They harm farm animals as well as humans.

Despite these and other nasty habits, flies and mosquitoes do play an important role on Earth. Without their assistance in pollination, certain plants and crops wouldn't reproduce. They are also sources of food for other animals, like mosquito-eating fish.

Is this fly about to fly?

Mosquitoes and flies are members of the order Diptera, or true flies, which contains 120,000 species. The oldest fly fossil is about 225 million years old, and one out of every ten animals classified today is a fly. Flies undergo complete metamorphosis. Their larvae are known by a number of names, including maggots or wrigglers.

The major thing that distinguishes all Diptera from other insects is that they all have only one set of true wings that can be used for flying. Their other set have become halteres. These small, clublike organs vibrate during flight and are used by flies to help them keep their balance.

THE WINTER CRANE FLY UNLIKE OTHER INSECTS IS A LARVA IN SUMMER AND BECOMES AN ADULT IN WINTER IT IS SO SENSITVE TO WARMTH THAT THE TOUCH OF A HUMAN'S WARM HAND MAY KILL IT

The female Hessian fly sends out a tempting aroma to attract males.

Shoo, Fly!

Flies can be found just about everywhere and so can their larvae. Fly larvae are in the ground, in the water, and on plants and animals. The larvae of one species live in hot springs and geysers. Larvae of another species live in pools of crude oil.

Most flies and fly larvae will eat just about everything, including plants and plant nectar, animals, carrion (decaying flesh), dung, and even other flies.

These maggots, also known as fly larvae, are used as fish bait!

Do you like your flies supersized?

Flies in Flight

Flies are among the best fliers in the insect kingdom. They can fly forward and backward, turn in place, and hover. They have one of the highest wing beat frequencies of any animal; some species beat their wings 1,000 times per second. The characteristic buzzing noise you hear from some flies is the noise their wings make. You can only hear this buzzing when flies get older and the speed of their wings slows down.

Flies are not always pests. They also play an important role in pollinating plants.

Flies can't actually fly upside down, but they can land on a ceiling. They do this by flipping their bodies around in midair.

Houseflies at Home

Ninety-eight percent of the flies you catch in your house are houseflies. Their larvae feed on garbage and any food you leave around. Adult houseflies feed on food, too. The problem with houseflies is that their feet can carry diseases like cholera, typhoid, and dysentery.

This view of a housefly shows its clear wings held back.

Believe It or Not!
IT ONLY TAKES 60 DAYS for a HOUSEFLY TO BECOME A GREAT GRANDMOTHER!

IN SIX MONTHS OVER 330 TRILLION HOUSEFLIES CAN DEVELOP from a SINGLE BREEDING PAIR!

No adult fly can chew, though fly larvae can and do. The mouthparts of adult flies are designed to pierce and/or suck, lick, or sponge up food.

Our Fly Friends

There are some "good guys" in the fly universe. Dung flies live only in dung and help clean up the environment by eating it. Hover fly larvae eat aphids, making them very useful to gardeners. Hover flies, which look a lot like wasps, are the second most important group of insect pollinators, after bees and wasps.

Pomace flies, also known as vinegar or fruit flies, can be agricultural pests, destroying a variety of crops (primarily fruits). But the best known species of pomace fly, *Drosophila melanogaster*, has been used extensively by humans for the study of biology and genetics. That's because these flies have a very short life span—two weeks—and each female lays about 2,000 eggs. That adds up to a lot of fruit flies for entomologists to study. Pomace flies have also been used to control certain weeds.

The coloring and hovering, darting movements of hover flies mimic that of bees and wasps.

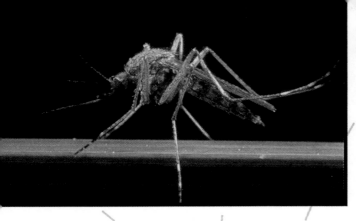

Does this mosquito look innocent? Keep in mind that of all insects, the mosquito may be the most harmful to humans. This is because some of them transmit serious diseases.

Mosquito Mania

There are about 2,500 species of mosquitoes throughout the world. Mosquito wings have scales, while wings of other flies do not. The male mosquito's principal food source is nectar and other sugary liquids.

Male mosquitoes find females by the sound of their wings beating. (Females beat their wings at a different speed from males.) Females lay their eggs in still or slow-moving pools of water. Mosquitoes undergo complete metamorphosis; their larvae and pupae develop in the water. The larvae eat algae, plankton, fungi, bacteria, and other microorganisms that live there. They come up to the surface regularly to breathe. In their pupal stage, they actually float on the top of the water, where they take oxygen in through two air tubes called "trumpets," which work a little like snorkels do. After the larvae hatch, they rest on the water while their bodies and wings dry and harden.

Some mosquito species attach a group of eggs into a mosquito "raft" that can consist of 200 to 300 eggs. Others lay their eggs one at a time.

THE WINGS of FEMALE MOSQUITOES BEAT 500 TIMES A SECOND!

FLAP FLAP FLAP

Ouch!

Only female mosquitoes bite. They do it because they need protein for their eggs to develop properly. First, the mosquito uses her mouthparts to pierce a hole in your skin. Then she uses a long, piercing mouthpart called a stylet, which is like a little, hollow needle, to suck up your blood. In the meantime, her saliva prevents your blood from coagulating, or thickening. If it coagulated, it wouldn't go up the stylet, and the mosquito wouldn't get her meal. It is an allergic reaction to mosquito saliva that causes the red, raised, itchy bump you get when you're bitten.

A mosquito on human skin. Uh-oh! Looks like her abdomen's already filled up with blood!

Interacting with Insects

Insects have been interacting with other inhabitants of Earth for millions of years. Often, both parties benefit. Other times, it's a more one-sided relationship.

A parasitic wasp is about to immobilize a boll weevil larva for her own nourishment as well as for that of her developing eggs.

THE JEWELWEED PRODUCES HONEY DEW FROM ITS LEAVES

THE SECRETION ATTRACTS ANTS-WHICH PREVENT THE PLANT FROM BEING DEVOURED BY CATERPILLARS

Flower nectar and pollen is the bumblebee's food of choice.

Gotcha! While the Mexican bean beetle larvae are enjoying a meal, along comes a predatory stinkbug. The diners become the dined upon!

The Insect/Plant Connection

For more than 300 million years, plants have been providing insects with sources of food and places to live and reproduce. In return, plants use insects to ensure their own survival. Some insects pollinate a plant so it can produce seeds and new plants. Other insects eat plants to keep the plant population the right size. Still others protect plants from more destructive predators.

When flowering plants developed more than 100 million years ago, an even more special relationship was born between plants and insects. Insects evolved to better serve these flowering plants. And flowers evolved to better communicate with insects. They became brightly colored and just the right size and shape to attract insects. They began to emit chemicals, which sometimes smell sweet, to signal insects that it's time for a visit.

Some plants "learned" to give off chemicals when they're under attack to call for insect help. Attacking caterpillars, for instance, cause plants to emit a certain chemical. Special parasitic wasps pick up these signals and rush to the rescue. They implant their eggs into the caterpillars, and when the eggs hatch, the wasp larvae eat the caterpillars from the inside out. Other plants send out chemicals that discourage the wrong kind of insect from visiting.

Sometimes, plants work together to support insects' needs. Many plants flower late in the season so that insects that live through the winter can get a "sugar fix" before cold weather sets in. The following spring, the same insects might visit different plants that flower early to provide the insects with the proper diet for egg development. In this way, early and late-flowering plants can use the same insect pollinators but serve different needs of the insects.

These yellow-necked caterpillars appear to be taking a lunch break!

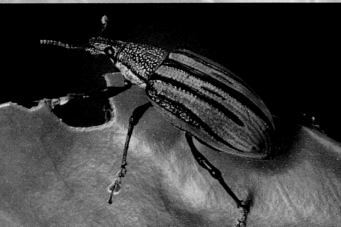

Munch, munch. Besides citrus trees, this adult citrus root weevil also likes to munch on potatoes, sugarcane, papaya, and lots of vegetables.

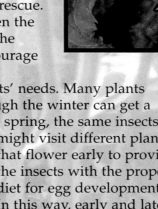

The gypsy moth caterpillar is the greatest forest and shade tree pest in the northeastern United States.

Some flowers actually open at certain times during the day to make it easier for bees to feed on them.

47

Insect-to-Insect

There are many examples of interesting relationships between insects, even between different species. Some ants rear aphids for their honeydew. Others harvest honeydew from mealybugs; in return, they help spread mealybug populations from plant to plant (not a very good deal for the plant, however, since mealybugs can be extremely destructive).

Ecuadorian ants help protect the larvae of treehoppers from predators in return for their honeydew secretions. Some species of butterfly actually "hire" ants as bodyguards. Their larvae secrete a liquid that's eaten by the ants. Some even "sing" to attract their ant bodyguards. In return, the ants guard them from predators and allow them to eat ant larvae. Colonies of bees, wasps, ants, and termites also have complicated and cooperative relationships.

Treehoppers produce honeydew, which some ants like to eat.

Members of ant colonies have the same "nest odor." If an ant from another colony—even if it's the same species—wanders into a "foreign" ant colony, it will be recognized as an intruder because of its odor and be attacked.

Tailor ants work together to build their nests by "sewing" leaves together.

Insects and Other Animals— Including Humans

The relationship between humans, animals, and insects often seems one-sided. That's because some insects bite or pierce animals (including us) to drink their blood. This blood is a necessary source of protein for their eggs.

Many of these insects, however, make up for drinking our blood in some very important ways. They control other insect pests. They pollinate food crops. (It's been estimated that if you paid the insects for the work they do on behalf of plants and humans, you'd have to fork out $17 billion every year!) They make products that people use, such as honey, beeswax, silk, shellac, and a number of different dyes. They help recycle organic matter and clean up the environment. They also serve as food for other creatures that people eat—as well as for people.

But despite their value, insects do sometimes become pests—at least from a human point of view. When they do, humans often deal with them by using insecticides. But insecticides—poisons that target insect populations—have many drawbacks. For one thing, they can pollute or even poison the environment. For another, they can kill beneficial insects. Also, insects quickly develop resistance to insecticides, so stronger ones are always needed.

A new biological control—the celery looper virus—is being tested against crop pests like this cotton bollworm. The virus is named after one of the insects it targets— the celery looper caterpillar.

An entomologist examines a leaf damaged by the tortoise beetle.

The saltcedar is an invasive plant that poses a threat to native plant communities. The United States is now attempting to control saltcedar by using a leaf beetle as a biological control agent.

Scientists have genetically engineered a variety of plants by incorporating Bt genes into them. Bt is a natural insecticide, and the hope is that such plants will be resistant to insect damage. But the process is controversial. It is feared by some that Bt crops could damage innocent insect species. And some insects have already become resistant to Bt crops.

Other Ways

Different ways of controlling insect populations other than chemical pesticides have been successful. One way is by using genetic controls. These include releasing sterile males into the environment to mate with females.

Another is by using cultural controls. These include growing special, pest-resistant varieties of crops and rotating crops—growing different crops from year to year, so insect pests that prey on specific crops need to migrate to survive.

A third is by using biological controls. These include using predator insects to help keep pest populations in check. A kind of ladybug beetle, for example, was successfully introduced into California citrus groves to control a pesky pest—the cottony cushion scale.

Believe It or Not! A POPULAR DISH in *Burma!* PORK-STUFFED CRICKET!

A lady beetle devours a pea aphid.

In 1991, delegates to a conference in South Africa were given a meal consisting of *LOCUSTS, TERMITES, WATER LILIES* and *CATERPILLARS IN PUFF PASTRY!*

Food for Thought

Lots of insects, like mosquitoes and black flies, have probably eaten bits of you. But you've probably eaten some insects, too. They might have been in a piece of fruit, or in your bread, or in your vegetables. Insect bits can be found in peanut butter, and while insect eggs and maggots have been known to show up in canned tomato sauce.

Before you make a face and decide never to eat anything again, it's worth noting that lots of people around the world eat insects on purpose. Insects can be a good source of food. People in Africa eat ants, worms, termites, and grasshoppers. In Nigeria, a west African country, they pan-fry large palm weevil grubs. Japan exports the pupae of silkworms as food. Mexico exports tinned caterpillars. In Thailand, especially in the north, people deep-fry grasshoppers and tree beetles, stir-fry giant water bugs, and munch on the eggs of the red ant. Yum!

Insects Under the Microscope

Meet a cockroach— head on!

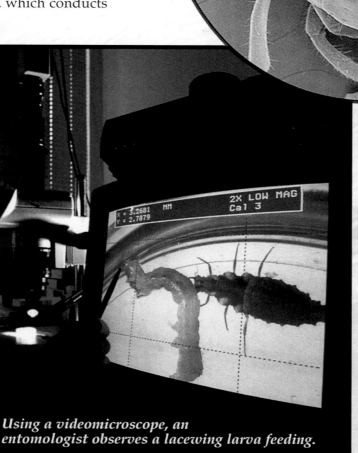

Every day, entomologists are learning more and more about incredible insects. One way they do this is by making use of amazing new equipment, such as the scanning electron microscope, or SEM for short.

Regular microscopes create magnified images by using glass lenses to bend light waves. SEMs use electrons—particles made up of a negative electrical charge—to magnify objects. SEMs create an image that is much more detailed and three-dimensional than the image that is created by a regular microscope.

Before they can be put into the SEM, samples of insects have to be prepared. First, the insect is carefully dried out so it doesn't shrivel up. Next, it's given a fine coating of gold, which conducts

SEM images originally were in black and white, but there is now equipment that allows these images to be seen in color.

Using a videomicroscope, an entomologist observes a lacewing larva feeding.

51

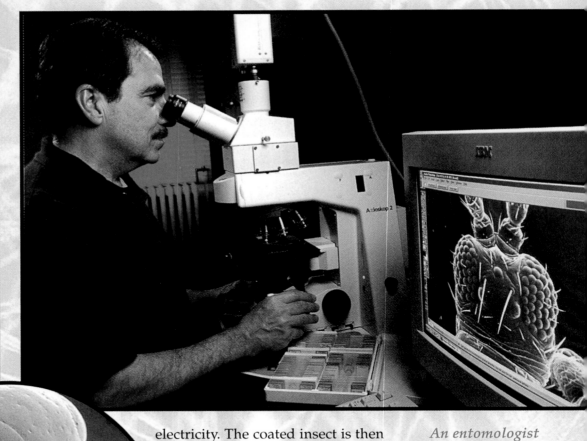

An entomologist uses magnification to compare an unidentified species of insect with a known species projected on a screen.

electricity. The coated insect is then placed inside the column of the microscope. All the air is pumped out, which creates a vacuum. Then an electron gun shoots a beam of high-energy electrons through a series of magnets that focus it into a kind of tiny "spotlight."

Near the bottom of the column, a set of coils move the "spotlight" back and forth across the insect. The beam knocks other electrons loose from the surface of the insect. Based on the number of electrons loosened from each spot the beam touches, an image of the insect is gradually built up.

A cockroach in profile, supersized!

A close-up view of a Hercules beetle's eye.

Wearing Wires

Entomologists are also devising other amazing ways to investigate insect behavior. At the Wye campus of the Imperial College in London, England, entomologists have actually managed to tie a fine gold wire to aphids and the plants they feed on. This creates an electrical circuit. When the aphid feeds, an electrical signal provides the entomologists with information about the aphid's feeding behavior.

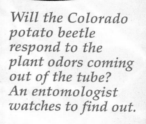

Will the Colorado potato beetle respond to the plant odors coming out of the tube? An entomologist watches to find out.

An entomologist prepares the antennae of a sawfly for electronic analysis.

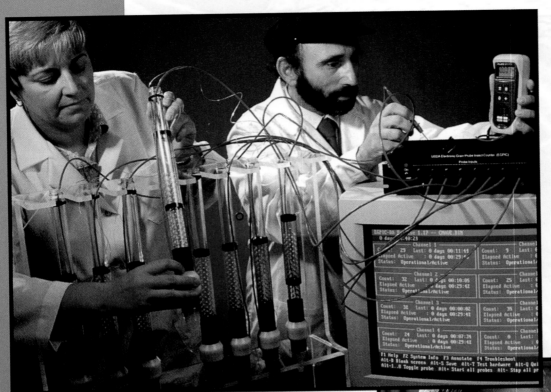

An entomologist collaborates with an electrical engineer to collect data on insects.

These entomologists also use a wind tunnel and an olfactometer—an instrument that can measure smells—to study how insects respond to chemical scents given off by plants. One study involves how some plants react when they are attacked by plant-eating insects. These plants fight back by attracting predators—or meat-eating insects—by sending out scent signals. The entomologists place predator insects in the wind tunnel and release scents given off by the plant into the airstream. They then study the insects' reaction to the scents. They've even attached insects' antennae to an electrical circuit to figure out which scents the insect is reacting to!

That's pretty extraordinary. But it's all in a day's work for the people who study these incredible insects.

How will corn earworm moths react to different mixtures of feeding stimulants and insecticides?

Discover More About Insects

Books About Insects

1001 Facts About Insects (Backpack Books) by Laurence Mound and Steve Brooks. Dorling Kindersley Publishing, 2003.

Broadsides from the Other Orders: A Book of Bugs by Sue Hubbell. Random House, 1993.

Bugs of the World by George C. McGavin. Blandford, an imprint of Cassell plc, 1993.

Insects and Spiders by Matthew Robertson. Readers' Digest Children's Books, 2000.

Insects & Spiders: An Explore Your World Handbook by the editors of Discovery Books/an imprint of Random House, 2000.

National Audubon Society Field Guide to North American Insects & Spiders by Lorus and Margery Milne. Chanticleer Press, Inc./Alfred A. Knopf, Inc., 1980.

The Science Times Book of Insects edited by Nicholas Wade. The New York Times, 1998.

Smithsonian Handbooks: Insects, Spiders, and Other Terrestrial Arthropods by George C. McGavin. Dorling Kindersley Publishing, 2002.

Besides the books listed above, you can find many other books about insects, as well as guides to collecting insects. Check your local library. The librarian will probably be able to help you find what you need. Or do some research online.

Local cooperative extensions, also known as agricultural extensions, may be able to provide information about local insect populations. These organizations exist to help farmers and gardeners, and their phone numbers can be found in your local telephone book.

Check out your local natural history museums. Many of them have sections devoted to insects, such as:

- The Butterfly Conservatory at the Museum of Natural History in New York City

- The Field Museum Butterfly Collection in Chicago

- The Science Museum of Minnesota in St. Paul

- The Butterfly Habitat Garden at the Smithsonian's National Museum of Natural History in Washington, D.C.

There are even special insect museums, like The Katydid Insect Museum, in Glendale, Arizona. Look them up online or in your local yellow pages.

And if there aren't museums in your area, look online. Many have fascinating web sites. It's the next best thing to being there.

Mostly, keep your eyes and ears open! There are insects all around you.

Glossary

abdomen The rear section of an insect's body.

alates Reproductive male or female termites.

antennae A pair of slender, segmented sensory organs found on the heads of insects. Crustaceans, like lobsters and shrimp, also have antennae.

arthropods Animals that have exoskeletons—skeletons that are on the outside of their bodies, rather than on the inside, like bones.

boll The seedpod of a cotton plant.

camouflage Body colors or patterns that disguise an animal so predators cannot easily see it.

carbon dioxide One of the gases that make up air on Earth. People don't use carbon dioxide, so after they breathe in, they exhale it. Plants, on the other hand, use carbon dioxide for photosynthesis.

carnivorous An animal that eats only other animals.

chiton Part of the hard material that forms the exoskeleton and wings of an insect.

chrysalis The hard covering that protects the pupa of a butterfly.

cocoon A covering, usually of silk, that protects the pupa of an insect.

compound eyes Insect eyes that are made up of many different six-sided facets, which are also called eyelets.

electrons Tiny, negatively charged particles that are found in every atom.

elytra The hard front wings of beetles.

emit To give or send out.

entomologist A scientist who studies insects.

evolve To change over time.

exoskeleton A protective structure on the outside of an animal.

facets The sections of an insect's compound eyes.

formic acid A colorless acid found in many insects and plants.

gills Organs that can obtain oxygen from water.

halteres Small, clublike organs that were formerly the back wings of flies and mosquitoes and help stabilize these insects in flight.

hibernate To become inactive for a time, during which growth or development may take place.

invertebrates Animals that don't have a backbone.

larva The immature stage of an insect that is hatched from an egg, looks different from the adult insect, and undergoes complete metamorphosis.

mandibles One of the mouthparts of an insect.

olfactometer An instrument that can measure smells.

parasite An organism that lives on or in another organism and uses it without giving anything back in return.

pheromones Chemicals given off by one animal, usually to attract another of the same species.

pollinate To help a plant reproduce by carrying pollen from one plant to another, or from one part of a plant to another part of the same plant.

pore A tiny hole on the surface of an animal or plant.

predator An animal that preys on another animal for food.

proboscis The long tube that extends from the mouthparts of certain invertebrates (like butterflies) that enables them to feed.

prolegs The small, hooked "extra" legs on caterpillars than enable them to grip the plants they eat.

pupa The stage in which the larvae of insects that go through complete metamorphosis develop into adults.

segmented Divided into distinct sections.

sensilla The sense organs of insects.

spiracle An opening through which air can be let in and out.

stationary Not moving.

sterile An inability to reproduce. If a sterile insect mates with a fertile (one who can reproduce) insect, there will be no offspring.

stylet The thin, hollow tube that mosquitoes insert into a mammal to draw out its blood.

thorax The middle section of an insect's body.

tympanum A structure that allows insects to hear.

vacuum A space that's totally empty of matter, including air molecules.

wingspan The length from the tip of one wing to the tip of the other.

metamorphosis The changes an insect goes through while it's developing from egg to larva to fully-grown adult.

microorganism A tiny organism that can only be seen with the help of a microscope.

migrate To travel from one place to another for some reason—for example, to find food or better weather.

mimicry When an insect has evolved to look like another insect or something else in its environment, giving it additional protection from predators.

ocelli Simple insect eyes. Ocelli can only distinguish between light and dark.

Index

A

Abdomen 4, 25, 32
Alates 41
Aleoides indiscretus wasp 27
American cockroaches 6
Antennae 4, 11, 14, 26, 27, 28, 29, 53, 54
Ants 14, 15, 18, 19, 22, 32, 38, 39, 40, 46, 48, 50
Ant lions 43
Aphids 20, 21, 30, 44, 48, 50, 53
Aphthona flava flea beetle 31
Army ants 39
Arthropods 2, 3, 23
Assassin bug 16, 21

B

Backswimmer 10
Bees 2, 9, 11, 13, 15, 20, 22, 32, 33, 34, 35, 36, 40, 44, 47, 48
Beetles 3, 5, 8, 10, 19, 21, 22, 23, 29, 30, 31, 36, 46, 49, 50, 52, 53
Black flies 50
Blue orchard bee 32
Boll weevil 30, 46
Brachonid wasp 36
Budworm 31
Bugs 5, 16, 21, 30, 46
Bumblebee 32, 33, 46
Butterflies 8, 16, 17, 20, 22, 23, 24, 25, 26, 27, 28

C

Cabbage butterfly 27
Camouflage 17, 18
Carabid beetles 31
Carpenter bees 33
Caterpillars 7, 17, 18, 23, 25, 27, 31, 36, 46, 47, 49, 50
Cecropia moth 24
Celery looper caterpillars 49
Cerci 4
Chiton 8
Chrysalid 23, 25
Cicada killer wasp 19
Cicadas 14, 19, 22
Citrus root weevil 47
Click beetle 29
Cockroaches 4, 6, 7, 13, 16, 22, 51, 52
Cocoon 23, 25
Colorado potato beetle 21, 31, 53
Compound eye 4, 12
Convergent ladybug beetles 3
Corn earworm 32
Cotton bollworms 49 ·
Crane fly 42
Crickets 14, 22, 50
Crops 2, 27, 28, 30, 31, 42, 44, 49, 50

D

Damselflies 8, 22
Death-watch beetles 30

Desert ants 39
Digger wasps 36
Diseases 2, 44, 45
Diving beetles 10, 30
Downy leather-wings 31
Dragonflies 3, 4, 6, 8, 9, 10, 13, 20, 22
Drones 34, 38
Dung beetles 30
Dytiscid beetle 10

E

Earworm moths 54
Eastern spotted cucumber beetle 30
Ecuadorian ants 48
Elytra 8, 29, 30
Entomologists 3, 49, 51, 52, 53, 54
European red-bellied clerid beetle 31
Exoskeleton 6, 22, 29
Eyes 12, 13

F

Facets 12
Field bees 34, 35
Fire ants 19
Fireflies 12, 29
Fleas 9, 22
Flies 7, 8, 9, 12, 13, 14, 19, 21, 22, 23, 42, 43, 53

Formic acid 39
Formosan subterranean termites 40, 41
Fossil 6, 40, 42
Fruit flies (Pomace flies) 44

G

Glossy pillbugs 31
Glowworms 20
Goldsmith beetle 30
Goliath beetle 5
Grasshoppers 9, 16, 19, 22, 50
Great spangled fritillary butterfly 24
Green lacewing 23
Grubs 23
Gypsy moths 27, 31, 47

H

Halteres 9, 42
Hawk moth 17, 27
Hercules beetle 52
Hessian fly 42
Honey 33, 34
Honeybees 33, 35
Hornets 17, 37
Hornet clearwing moth 17
Horse fly 43
Houseflies 8, 9, 44
Hover flies 44

I

Inchworm caterpillar 7
Insecticides 49, 50, 54
Invertebrates 3
Io moth 17

J

Japanese beetles 30
Jewel wasps 36

K

Kamehameha butterfly 24
Karner blue butterfly 26
Katydids 14, 17

L

Ladybugs (lady beetles) 3, 29, 31, 50
Lange's metalmark butterfly 26
Larvae 19, 21, 23, 30, 31, 36, 39, 42, 43, 44, 45, 46, 48
Leaf-cutting ants 39
Leaf-footed bugs 16
Leaf beetles 49
Legs 4, 7, 9
Lice 7, 19
Locust 22, 50
Locust borer 31
Long-horned grasshoppers 16
Luna moth 27

M

Madagascan giant hissing roaches 4
Maggots 23, 42, 43, 50
Maize weevil 11
Mantises 2, 18, 22
Mason wasps 37
Mealworms 30

Mealybugs 48
Meganeura 6
Metallic green tiger beetle 30
Metamorphosis 22, 23, 29, 32, 40, 42, 45
Mexican bean beetle 46
Mexican fruit fly 21
Midge 9
Mimicry 17
Molting 22
Monarch butterflies 8, 16, 17, 24
Mourning clock butterfly 25
Mouthparts (mandibles) 4, 5, 19, 27, 30, 39, 45, 59
Mosquitoes 3, 4, 8, 11, 15, 22, 41, 45, 50
Moths 14, 15, 16, 17, 22, 23, 24, 25, 27, 28, 46, 54
Mustached mud bee 34

N

New Guinea walking stick 16
Nymphs 10, 22, 23, 40

O

Ocelli 13
Olfactometer 54
Osmia ribifloris bee 2
Owl butterfly 17

P

Painted lady butterfly 8
Paper wasps 37
Parasitic wasp 18, 46
Parnassian butterfly 28
Pea aphids 50
Pesticides 50
Pheromones 15, 41
Phorid flies 19
Pollination 31, 32, 41, 43, 47, 49

Polyphemus moth 16
Pomace flies 44
Pretarsus 7
Preying mantis 2, 18
Proboscis 26, 27
Pupae 23, 39, 45, 50

Q

Queen bee 33, 34

R

Reproduction 20

S

Sawfly 43, 53
Scanning electron microscope (SEM) 51
Screwworm 23
Sensilla 11, 14, 15
Shield bug 16, 21
Silk moth 15
Silkworm 50
Silverfish 22
Slugmoth caterpillars 25
South American army ants 39
Sphinx moth caterpillar 37
Spined soldier bug 46
Spiny oak slug moth 16
Spiracles 4
Springtails 22
Stag beetles 30
Stalk-eyed fly 13
Stick insects 17
Stingers 35, 36, 37
Stinkbug 5, 16, 21
Subterranean termites 41
Sugarcane borer 28
Swallowtail butterflies 26
Sweat bee 32

T

Tailor ants 48
Tarnished plant bug
Termites 38, 40, 41, 48, 50
Termite nests 40, 41
Thorax 4
Tiphid wasps 36
Tortoise beetles 49
Tree beetles 50
Treehoppers 48
Tumblebugs 30
Tympanum 14

V

Vedalia beetles 31

W

Walking sticks 16, 22
Wasps 4, 9, 11, 17, 18, 19, 22, 27, 32, 36, 37, 40, 44, 46, 47, 48
Water bugs 50
Water striders 10
Weevils 11, 30, 47, 50
Whirligig beetles 10
Whiteflies 23
Wings 4, 8, 9, 24, 25, 26, 29, 35, 40, 45
Winter crane fly 42
Wood ants 18
Wood-burrowing termites 40
Worms 50

Y

Yellow jackets 36, 37
Yellow-necked caterpillars 47

Photo Credits

t=top

tm=top middle

mr=middle right

br=bottom right

tl=top left

m=middle

b=bottom

tr=top right

ml=middle left

bl=bottom left

Ablestock
Page 43 (tl) © Ablestock Images

Agricultural Research Service, United States Department of Agriculture
Title page © Keith Weller
Page i (t) © Jack Dykinga
Page i (b) © Scott Bauer
Page 3 (tr) © Keith Weller
Page 3 (b) © Scott Bauer
Page 11 (b) © ARS
Page 18 (b) © Scott Bauer
Page 19 (t) © Sanford Peter
Page 19 (b) © Scott Bauer
Page 21 (t) © Jack Dykinga
Page 23 (t) © Jack Dykinga
Page 23 (b) © John Kucharski
Page 27 (b) © Scott Bauer
Page 28 © William White
Page 30 (b) © ARS
Page 31 (tl) © ARS
Page 31 (b) © Scott Bauer
Page 31 (tr) © Scott Bauer
Page 32 (tr) © Scott Bauer
Page 32 (bl) © Scott Bauer
Page 32 (br) © Scott Bauer
Page 34 (b) © Scott Bauer
Page 36 (b) © Scott Bauer
Page 40 (m) © Scott Bauer
Page 40 (t) © Scott Bauer
Page 41 (t) © Scott Bauer
Page 42 (b) © Scott Bauer
Page 43 (m) © Jason Stanley
Page 45 (b) © ARS
Page 46 (m) © Scott Bauer
Page 46 (b) © ARS
Page 47 (m) © Keith Weller
Page 49 (t) © Scott Bauer
Page 49 (m) © Peggy Greb
Page 49 (b) © Bob Richard, APHIS
Page 50 © Scott Bauer
Page 51 © Jack Dykinga
Page 52 © Peggy Greb
Page 53 © Keith Weller
Page 53 © Keith Weller
Page 54 © Stephen Ausmus
Page 54 © Scott Bauer

Classroom Clipart
Pages 15 (b), 35 (t), 37 (bl), 38 (t), (b), 44 (t) © Classroom Clipart

Corel Images
Pages 10 (t), (mr), (ml), 16 (t), 14 (t), 20 (l), 21 (b), 22 (t), (b), 24 (l), 25 (tl), (tm), (tr), (b), 27 (m), 28 (r), 29 (t), (bl), (br), 31 (bl), 32 (mr), 36 (t), 43 (b), 37 (t), (br), 45 (t), 47 (b), 48 (t) © Corel Images

United States Fish and Wildlife Services
Page 3 (l) © Walton LaVonda
Page 5 (m) © Paul Gertler
Page 8 (t) © John & Karen Hollingsworth
Page 8 (b) © Jon R. Nickles
Page 17 (b) © Glen Smart
Page 18 (t) © Gene Whitaker
Page 24 (t) © Ed Loth
Page 24 (b) © William Hartgroves
Page 26 (t) © Jerry Powell
Page 26 (m) © James C. Leupold
Page 26 (b) © John & Karen Hollingsworth
Page 28 (t) © William Radke
Page 34 (t) © Gary M. Stolz
Page 58 (b) © USFWS

Picturequest
Page 6 (b) © Creatas/Picturequest

Getty Images
Pages 1 (t), 2 (t), 5 (b), 7 (b), 9 (b), 13 (b), 16 (b), 17 (t), 21 (m), 33 (t), (b), 36 (b), 39 (b), 41 (b), 44 (b), 46 (t), 48 (b), 56 (b), 57 (l), 59 (t) © Getty Creative Images

Microscope and Graphic Imaging Center, California State University, Hayward
Pages 7 (t), 9 (t), 11 (t), 12 (m), 43 (tl) © Melissa Carter

Department of Entomology, University of California, Riverside
Page 52 (b) © David Hawks

Michigan State University
Page 39 (t) © Gerald R. Urquhart, Ph.D.

Charles Schurch Lewallen
Page 19 (b) © Charles Schurch Lewallen

Laura Miller
Page 13 (t) © Laura Miller

Ripley Entertainment Inc.
Page 17 (m) © Ripley Entertainment Inc.

Original Believe It or Not! ® Cartoons
Copyright page, pages 5, 6 (tr), (l), 9 (tr), (m), 10 (tr), 11 (b), 13 (tr), 14 (m), 15 (b), 16 (bl), 17 (m), 20 (b), 22 (l), 26 (br), 27 (tr), 35 (b), 37 (tl), 38 (bl), 39 (m), 40 (b), 42 (l), 44 (l), (r), 45 (m), 46 (m), 50 (t), (b), Used with permission of Ripley Entertainment Inc.